Well, Come to KLANADA

© *2014, 2020*

WELL, COME TO KLANADA

BY
GRAND SHEIK BROTHER KUDJO ADWO EL
MOORISH SCIENCE TEMPLE OF AMERICA
CANAANLAND - TORONTO

EDITED BY
SIS. TAUHEEDAH S. NAJEE-ULLAH EL
MOORISH SCIENCE TEMPLE CALIFORNIA, INC.

Visit califamedia.com for member discounts and freebies

© 2014

A Moorish Guide Publishing Company
cmcanaanland@gmail.com

Table of Contents

Preface 1

I.   First Canadians 2

II. CANADA, INC. 5

III. Slavery Hidden As Indenture. 14

IV. Dred Scott Decision 19

V.   Too Cold For Blacks 21

VI. Our Authority 24

VII. The Power of Persuasion 26

VIII. Canadian Common Wealth 27

IX. Moor's Head 31

Biblio-/Discography 32

Index 34

Preface

ANNEX
1. To add or join to; append or attach, ESPECIALLY TO A LARGER OR MORE SIGNIFICANT THING. 2. To INCORPORATE (territory) into an existing country or state.– (American Heritage Dictionary 1969)

ANNEXATION
A process in International Law which consists of removing the enemies flag, hoisting the conquerors' flag and reading a proclamation that proclaims that the land has been formerly annexed.
(Amir: Heru Ranesi El 2010)

10. *And it shall be, when the Lord thy God shall have brought thee into the land which he sware unto thy fathers, to Abraham, to Isaac and to Jacob, to give thee great and goodly cities, which thou buildedest not, 11. And houses all of good things, which thou filledst not, and wells digged which thou diggedst not, vineyards and olive trees, which thou planedst not; when thou shalt eaten and be full:*
Deuteronomy Chapter 6, Verse 10-11 (The Holy Bible n.d.)

I. First Canadians

Most anthropologists believe Canada's first immigrants used a natural land bridge called Beringia to reach North America. The Bering land bridge (Bering Strait) is significant because it is believed to have enabled human migration to the Americas from Asia at least 15,000 years ago but we have been on this Continent before there *was* an Atlantic ocean. Most scholars believe that these ancient ancestors of modern Native Americans migrated to the Americas from northeastern Asia. The Original Man, founders of civilization includes all nonwhite people, and is also termed Asiatic. Asiatic denotes the true heritage of the Melanin Being. Prophet Noble Drew Ali taught that Moors were "Asiatic", that there are only two races on the planet, Europeans and Asiatics. The peoples of Africa, Indigenous peoples of America and the Pacific, as well as Latin Americans, are all considered Asiatic, as well as Moslems, (not Muslims) in Moorish Science Temple teachings. Though so many have been deliberately destroyed, over 200,000 ancient pyramids and huge mounds of earth in the shape of cones, animals and geometric designs can still be found from the southern coast of America to Canada. Moors lived in North America long before Europeans came; it was called North Amexem. Northwest Amexem had 5 Ancient Great Lakes, which was part of the Al Moroccan Empire. They supplied fresh water to the civilizations of the Americas. These lakes were Atomic Lakes, Lacus Atomus, These Great Lakes are Michigan, Ontario, Erie, Huron and Superior. Canaan Land was the name of the habitable part of Northern Northwest Amexem.

"Black Canadians were in Canada from the earliest times, initially as free people, then as slaves." (Services 2011).

"The Washitaw never drew boundaries. We are the original inhabitants of all the lands from the Atlantic to the Pacific, down through Muu (South America). Wherever you find a Washitaw family or Washitaw mound site, you find part of the Empire. In "said" North America, the area from the Alleghenies to the Rocky Mountains, from <u>CANADA</u> down to the Gulf of Mexico, including East and West Floridas; and west to the Pecos River, encompasses the domain of the Empire Washitaw de Dugdamoundya" (Shabazz Bey 1996)

"Evidence for black-skinned natives in the Americas long before the arrival of Columbus is abundant. From the distinctly negroid features of colossal Olmec sculpted heads and a pre-Aztec obsidian bowl being upheld by a figure with unmistakably black characteristics, to the bones of negroid persons excavated from a 2,000 year-old mound in northern Wisconsin, a wealth of material exists to establish the certainty of non-White, non-Indian population living in pre-Columbian America along with these other groups." (Issue 17 n.d.)

Our nation had its own myths, heroes, and spiritual practices and revered nature and a sense of the spiritual presence in all living things. There were approximately 600 diverse Tribal groups in Northwest Amexem. The first Indigenous people that inhabited the area of Ontario were the Great Mound Builders called the Adena People. The Adena people were kin to the Olmec civilizations of South America. The Washitaw are descendants of the Olmecs. Studies support a human presence in northern Yukon from 26,500 years ago, and in southern Ontario from 9,500 years ago. Vikings, Nordic peoples—Danes, Swedes, and Norwegians—who raided and settled in large areas of eastern and Western Europe during a period of Scandinavian expansion began to visit the northeast coast of Canada about AD 985. In the late 1700's, France took claim to a vast area bordering the American Colonies from the Great Lakes and the Ohio River valley southward to the Gulf of Mexico through ANNEXATION. England came to realize that the easiest riches of the New World, which in REALITY WAS THE MOORISH EMPIRE, were to be found in furs rather than in gold. So to put claim to the fur country, the Hudson's Bay Company was founded in 1670. Queen Anne's War (series colonial wars between France and Great Britain in North America for control of the continent), broke out in 1702 and led to the capture of Port Royal by the English in

1710. The Treaty of Paris of 1763 ended the Seven Years' War and Britain emerged as the world's leading colonial empire after using enormous book burnings and murdering of Indigenous people through SUBJUGATION to claim the Moorish Empire. Her annexed possessions were Hindustan (India) to Asia Soor (Africa) to Southwest Amexem (South America) to Northwest Amexem (North America). The British also took from France the so called "barren wasteland" misnomer Canada (which is Canaanland Republic of the Al Moroccan Empire) rather than prosperous West Indian sugar islands of Guadeloupe and Martinique. France chose to keep its Caribbean Islands and to leave its "North American" colony, "New France", to Britain. Loyalists and American colonists of varied ethnic backgrounds supported the British cause during the AMERICAN REVOLUTION (1775-83). In 1783, many thousands of Loyalists left the newly created United States.

II. CANADA, INC.

We must understand that when the history books say United States during the 1700's they are speaking of the United States Republic. The Republic is a constitutional form of government created by the people. The allies of the British started their lives afresh under the British flag in Nova Scotia and in the unsettled lands above the St. Lawrence rapids and north of Lake Ontario. Forests west of the Bay of Fundy—at one time part of French Acadia—were included in Nova Scotia and in the late 1800's were established as a separate colony known as New Brunswick. In 1791 the British Parliament enacted the Constitutional Act, whereby Quebec was split into the two provinces of Upper and Lower Canada. In 1840 the Act of Union was passed, became effective in 1841. This act joined Upper (Ontario) and Lower Canada (Quebec) under a central government. The two colonies were to be known simply as Canada. This is how the fiction of corporate state CANADA was created.

"The Act of Union's main provisions were the establishment of a single parliament with equal representation from each constituent section; consolidation of debt; a permanent Civil List; banishment of the French language from official government use; and suspension of specific French Canadian institutions relating to education and civil law." (British Parliament 1840)

The Act naturally aroused considerable opposition.

Following several constitutional conferences, the British North America Act brought about Confederation creating a "one Dominion under the name of Canada" with four provinces: Ontario, Quebec, Nova Scotia, and New Brunswick. In 1898, after the Klondike Gold Rush in the Northwest Territories, the Canadian government decided to create the Yukon Territory as a separate territory in the region to better control the situation. Canada is a constitutional monarchy with Elizabeth II, Queen of Canada, as head of state; the monarch of Canada also serves as head of state of fifteen other Commonwealth countries, putting Canada in a personal union relationship with those other states.

The British North America Act, 1867, Section 2 states:

2. The provisions of this Act referring to Her Majesty the Queen (Victoria) extend also to the heirs and successors of Her majesty, Kings and Queens of the United Kingdom of Great Britain and Ireland. (The British North America Act 1867).

The Statutes Revision Act repealed Section 2 of the BNA Act 1867. If this part was repealed that means there is no lawful declaration of authority for any heirs or successors to assume a monarchal position over Canada.

Acknowledging the Queen of Great Britain as Queen of Canada when it is only an honourary position. Moors, though unconscious, are being prosecuted, jailed and fined in the name of this Queen. This is why REGINA is the plaintiff against all "DEFENDANTS". The office of CROWN of CANADA is an ACTING OFFICIAL STATUS that OFFICERS of the COURT use to hide behind while exercising the continual deliberate TORTS against the Indigenous people of Northwest Amexem.

Figure 1 Noble Prophet Drew Ali

Remember, a "right" is forever; a "privilege" is given and can or will be taken away by the granting authority.

The British government created a pseudo-republican government for Canada under a DEMOCRACY which is our current Parliamentary system. Government is by an absolute dictator, a Governor General through the Crown by the British Monarchy. Sovereignty rested in him under COLOUR OF AUTHORITY. NO legitimate governments have existed at the Federal or Provincial levels in Canada.

"To God's People, governments are servants."

"Men being by nature all free, equal, and independent, no one can be put out of this estate and subjected to the power of another without his consent. The only way whereby anyone divests himself of his natural liberty and puts on the bonds of civil society is by agreeing with other men to join and unite into a community."
-Lord Monck 1st Governor General of Canada

"A confederation is a union of independent and sovereign states bound together by a pact or a treaty for the observance of certain conditions dependent upon the unanimous consent of the contracting parties, who are free to withdraw from the union."
-Dr. Ollivier Law Clerk House of Commons

The British North America Act, enacted by the Imperial Parliament, carried out neither the spirit nor the terms of the Quebec resolutions. The Quebec resolutions called for a Federal Union not a UNITED COLONY. The Parliament of Canada became a CENTRAL LEGISLATURE of a UNITED COLONY whose only power is to aid the Governor General, the agent of the Imperial Parliament. The BNA Act WAS NOT A CONSTITUTION but an ACT pulling the 4 colonies into the Dominion of Canada without Sovereign authority. The only authority in Canada resides in the British Monarchy.

"I think we have got to get away from the idea that the British North America Act is a contract "or treaty". I do not want to go into that, but it is true neither in history nor in law. The British North America Act is a statute, and has always been interpreted as a statute." Dr. W.P.M Kennedy, Prof. At Law UFT.

Statute of Westminster on December 11, 1931

Provinces were made Sovereign in Act 7 of this statute, free and independent, but since Canada has not acted on this by adopting a constitution, signing agreements we know that it is the power of the Act which is naught why these things were not done when the Statue of Westminster was enacted. Canada is a colonial possession of the British Monarchy and is not obligated to the people. **There can be no constitution in Canada, whether it is on the basis of the British North America Act or any other act, until the people of Canada accept it.** They have not accepted it. The Parliament of Canada is acting on assumed power and authority. Parliament "ratifying (confirmation of an Act, approval of a Treaty)" a treaty or agreement cannot take place as it is the Crown that signs and ratifies on behalf of the subordinate Parliament.

"I think the time is ripe for a change in the constitution. I do not think you would need much publicity in order to draw to the attention of the people of this country that the British North America Act is inadequate." - Dr. Beauchesne, special committee on BNA Act

Ever since December 11, 1931, the provinces have been living common-law with Ottawa and have the right to terminate this arrangement at any time they wish. Each of the provinces of Canada has been a completely sovereign and independent state, and because the provinces have signed nothing since then constituting a Federal Union and a Federal Government, and because no such treaty has been ratified by the people of Canada, the provinces still enjoy the status of sovereignty and are privileged to use it in any way they see fit.

"In the first place we know that every individual state was an individual sovereignty - that each had its own army and navy and political organization - and when they formed themselves into a confederation they only gave the central authority certain specific rights appertaining to sovereign powers. The dangers that have risen from this system we will avoid if we can agree upon forming a strong central government - a great Central Legislature - a constitution for a Union which will have all the rights

of sovereignty except those that are given to the local governments. Then we shall have taken a great step in advance of the American Republic"

-John A McDonald   1864 Halifax

For the major part, the Residuary Powers (Clipped Sovereignty) in Canada were granted to the federal government whereas in the Republic those powers were reserved to the States and the People. The people in order to be sovereign MUST be, in our case, Indigenous to the land.

Note:

US Securities and Exchange Commission has CANADA is listed as a corporation under CANADA (0000230098) business office

Canadian Embassy
1746 Massachusetts Ave NW
Washington, DC 20036.

"It is to be remembered that it was an obvious design [by the] Fathers of Confederation to reverse the process at work in the United States (States Rights) and to empower the central government of Canada with all of the powers necessarily incidental to national sovereignty. It appeared to the Fathers of Confederation that it was the weakness of the "center" which was the major defect of the American constitution and they determined that we needed to strengthen ours to avoid the difficulties (civil war) in which the Americans were found at the time when Canadian federalism was being drafted. "

- Claude Bélanger

So-Called "Underground Railroad Map"

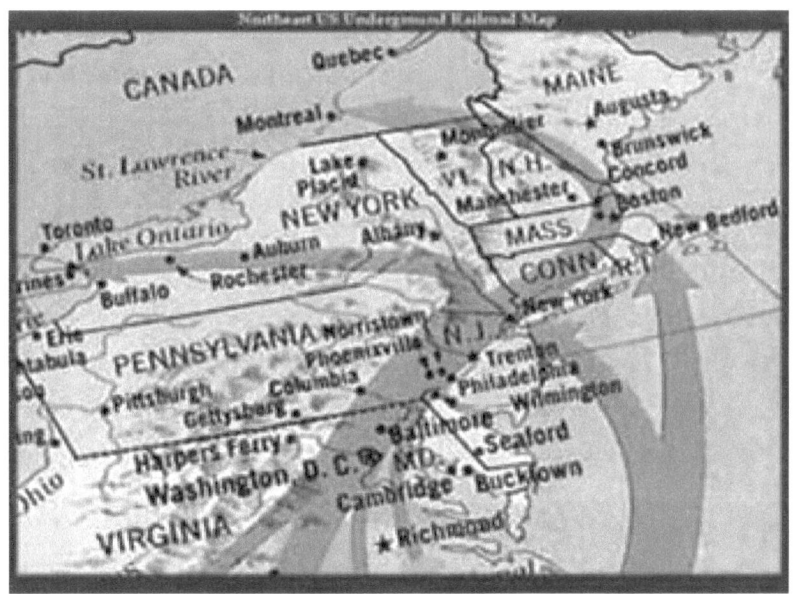

We were not slaves, but prisoners of war.

"Many distinguished persons were slave owners, including Peter Russell, who held positions in the executive and legislative councils and became administrator of Upper Canada; Secretary William Jarvis; and Upper Canada's first Solicitor General, Colonel James Gray. Indeed, six of the sixteen legislators in the first Parliament of Upper Canada were slave owners."- Daniel G. Hill

"Following the custom of the time he was a slaveholder, and in the early part of March, 1811, he (William Jarvis, who Jarvis Collegiate is named after) complained to the court that a negro boy and girl, his slaves, had stolen silver and gold from a desk at his house and escaped from their master, and that they had been aided and advised by one Coachly, a free negro. The accused having been caught, the court ordered that the boy, named Henry, but commonly known as Prince, be committed to prison; that the girl be returned to her master, and Coachly be discharged." (Robertson 1894)

It is estimated that between 1850 and 1863, the Underground Railroad movement was responsible for helping approximately 70,000 slaves escape and journey safely northwards into Canada and subsequent freedom. Frederick Douglass said he knew of major stations in Albany, Syracuse, Rochester, Buffalo, and in Canada, St. Catharine's, and Ontario. The national Park Services conducted a study in 1990 with experts in historic preservations, African history, and US history and the most important findings of the study include the following:

- The Underground Railroad story is nationally significant.
- Elements of the story are represented in existing units and other sites, but many important resource types are not adequately represented and protected.
- Many sites remain that meet established criteria for designation as national historic landmarks.
- Many sites are in imminent danger of being lost or destroyed.
- There is a tremendous amount of interest in the subject, but little organized coordination and communication among interested individuals and organizations.
- Some sites have very high potential for preservation and visitor use.

- No single site or route completely reflects and characterizes the Underground Railroad. The story and resources involve networks and regions rather than individual sites and trails.
- A variety of partnership approaches would be most appropriate for the protection and interpretation of the Underground Railroad. These partnerships could include the federal, state, and local governments along with a variety of private sector involvement.

Britain supposedly outlawed the Slave Trade with the Slave Trade Act in 1807 and abolished Slavery in 1833 with the Slavery Abolition Act, but we are here discussing mentally an Underground Railroad slave escape system that happened 30 years after slavery was to be stopped. The Spanish, or betrayer Moors of the 1492 fall of the Moorish Empire in Granada, along with the Portuguese, continued the Slave Trade to an even greater extent. The Union States (U.S Democracy) "abolished" the slave trade the same time as England. Under the cover of Moorish tribal flags, the British became partners in the upcoming adventures of annexation and usurpation in recapturing the escaped Prisoners of Wars fleeing further into the Land of their Ancestors. The Slavery Abolition Act was repealed under the Statutes Law (Repeals) Act in 1998.

Only slaves below the age of six were freed as all slaves were redesignated as apprentices and fell under 3 classes

1. Slaves who were employed in Agriculture on Lands of their owners.

2. Slaves who were employed in Agriculture on Lands not belonging to their owners.

3. Slaves who were not part of the first 2 classes.

The 3rd class was released from "apprenticeships" on Aug 1st 1838 and the other 2 classes released Aug 1st 1840.

Thirteen British Colonies established and were recognised as the United States of America. Recognized internationally first by Great Britain (Treaty of Paris 1783) as it was them, Great Britain, the U.S.A was Declaring their Independence from and second, but more importantly by Morocco (Treaty of Peace and Friendship 1787). Great Britain, France and other colonialist powers were fighting for the territory of the Al

Moroccan Empire North, South and Central Amexem. The Jay Treaty 1794 (Treaty of London 1794), between Great Britain and United States of America averted another war due to issues from the American revolution. The Treaty was proclaimed in effect 1796. War Debts were settled by annexing land that was Annexed from Indigenous People. The Treaty applies to His Majesty's Subjects, and to the Citizens of the United States, and the Indigenous people dwelling on EITHER side of the said boundary line. The U.S Canada boundaries were created through arbitration and the treaty broke down because of John Jay eliminating the issue of compensation to slave owners for slaves, causing the War of 1812. The British ran out the French and maintained erroneous ties with the Union States Democratic Knights Templars, not the US Republic or its Citizens and had Canada erected by 1867. Canada was created AFTER prisoners of wars, between the European wars in North America, were using the so called "Underground Railroad" to "escape" slavery in the South. In 1870 Canada under The British obtained Northwestern Territories. Manitoba was admitted to Canada in 1870 after negotiation with Metis Provisional Government, WHO WERE NOT INDIGENOUS and not holding lawful title to negotiate with foreigners on the topic of Indigenous Land.

III. Slavery Hidden As Indenture.

The word slave was rarely used however, the preferred phrase being servant or Negro servant, which didn't matter since the title of the Negro didn't protect them from the harsh reality of servitude. Indentured servants could be punished as slaves and were subject to the most humiliating mistreatment. Due to poverty and no laws to protect them, Black loyalist became <u>bonded</u> due to last resorts or vagrancy. Melanin beings in Canada were abused through <u>trick contracts</u>, in which slaves were tricked into signing contracts that said 1 year term but meant longer in many cases. Many would arrange some way of getting their servants out of the province to permanent slavery in the West Indies. Since the word "Black" wasn't given much weight in the courts, the master had little fear of repercussions. "Blacks" received harsh sentences for minor crimes while whites would typically receive a fine. A Slave would be sentenced to 350 lashes for stealing a couple of small items then indentured for years as time to fit the CRIME. Free "blacks" often had trouble getting their fair share of provisions. Many had to indenture themselves to Europeans so their provisions were drawn by the master or the company for which they worked. The Black Loyalists had been promised good farmland but not only did most never receive their due, many black settlements were erected on poor, uneven land. In Early Canada many Europeans thought that blacks were natural slaves, suited only for brute labor and taking orders.

CODE NOIR

We must innerstand that slavery is a business between corporations. Slavery is a business with corporations transacting trade with goods called chattel property. Negro, Black, Coloured, Indian, Native and other misnomers for melanin free will beings are considered chattel property. It matters not what you think is fact, truth is what is fact. Until 1789, slaves in Canada were policed by an edict called Code Noir. Code Noir defined the conditions of slavery in the French colonial empire called New France. Through the Code Noir slaves had no rights and were subject to whatever conditions the master placed on the enslaved. Black Codes is associated with legislation passed by Southern states after the Civil War in an attempt to control labor, movement and activities of Indigenous People. This was in 1865, in the United States, but the Code Noir was 180 years before in Canada. The edict for Code Noir was passed in **1685**.

Excerpts From Code Noir 1685

Louis, by the grace of God, King of France and Navarre: to all those here present and to those to come,

GREETINGS. In that we must also care for all people that Divine Providence has put under our tutelage, we have agreed to have the reports of the officers we have sent to our American islands studied in our presence. These reports inform us of their need for our authority and our justice in order to maintain the discipline of the Roman, Catholic, and Apostolic Faith in the islands. Our authority is also required to settle issues dealing with the condition and quality of the slaves in said islands. We desire to settle these issues and inform them that, even though they reside infinitely far from our normal abode, we are always present for them, not only through the reach of our power but also by the promptness of our help toward their needs. For these reasons, and on the advice of our council and of our certain knowledge, absolute power and royal authority, we have declared, ruled, and ordered, and declare, rule, and order, that the following pleases us:

ARTICLE II. All slaves that shall be in our islands shall be baptized and instructed in the Roman, Catholic, and Apostolic Faith. We enjoin the inhabitants who shall purchase newly-arrived Negroes to inform the Governor and Intendant of said islands of this fact within no more than eight days, or risk being fined an arbitrary amount.

ARTICLE XXXIII. The slave who has struck his master in the face or has drawn blood, or has similarly struck the wife of his master, his mistress, or their children, shall be punished by death

ARTICLE XXXVIII. The fugitive slave who has been on the run for one month from the day his master reported him to the police, shall have his ears cut off and shall be branded with a *fleur de lys* on one shoulder. If he commits the same infraction for another month, again counting from the day he is reported, he shall have his hamstring cut and be branded with a *fleur de lys* on the other shoulder. The third time, he shall be put to death.

Branding

Moorish Ma Star teachers expose the branding fiction with their stories of capture and torture of Prisoners of War. Disfiguring and cutting off body parts was done as means of expressing anger for the Abolition of slavery, but those who kept slavery alive after the abolishment needed a branding system that will "Scar without the Scar". Those who refused to convert to Christianity were branded as said in the Code Noir. Loss of profits occurred when masters realized the branding and disfiguring "damaged the goods". This was when it was decided, the new BRAND will be with words, more so the family names of their captors in order to effectively defeat the Indigenous people of Amexem. This branding system expanded and systems had to be set up to distinguish Negro Slaves from enslaved Moors.

NEGROES AND FREE MEN

"To attain the end proposed, so far as might be within the reach of the Association, the following plan, with regard to the treatment of the blacks, was adopted:

I. They must be treated as Freemen.

II. As such they must earn their livelihood as we do, and not be dependent on charity.

III. Their labor must be performed under a well-organized superintendence.

IV. They will receive compensation for their labor, in the shape of daily wages, reserving a sufficient percentage to defray the cost of superintendence.

V. As soon as their labor shall be organized, they will be required to provide their own support.

VI. In the meanwhile, and until their earnings shall provide the means of their support, they will be aided with food, clothing, and shelter, but such supplies shall be charged to them as advances, to be paid by the receiver, without interest.

VII. They may erect tenements on the land, and occupy them, free of charge, but when they occupy tenements erected or supplied by the Association, they shall pay rent.

VIII. Schools and churches shall be established among them, and the sick be cared for.

IX. No idlers will be allowed among them, but all must work who can.

X. Each one will be encouraged to raise on his own ground such articles of food as his family may require, and be so taught gardening as to raise quantities for the army and navy and other markets.

XI. To guard against imposition upon their ignorance and inexperience, no stores will be allowed among them except those licensed by the Association.

In 1864 "black" voters protested against a city councilor who called us NIGGERS. European Canadians, through fear of mass migrations from the South after the emancipation proclamation excluded "black" children from school and refused to assist the Freedman's Relief Association. The Association was organized in New York in 1862 to make a special appeal to the public, to appoint suitable teachers to instruct the Freedmen in industrial and mechanical arts, in the rudiments of education, the principles of Christianity, their accountability to the laws of God and man, their relation to each other as social beings, and all that might be necessary to render them competent to sustain themselves as members of a civilized society.

NOTE: Free White persons in the Naturalization Act, 1870, included European Jews, Moorish inhabitants of Spain and Portugal, mixed Greek, Latin, Phoenician and North African inhabitants of Italy. IT DOES NOT MEAN CAUCASIAN, ARYAN, OR INDO EUROPEAN RACES.

When so called "slaves" were freed in 1865 former Confederate soldiers had already founded the Ku Klux Klan to keep Moors form coming into their own by use of intimidation and violence to keep "slaves" segregated. The Freedman's Bureau was formed in 1865 to provide needed medical, legal and social assistance to the subjugated Moors now emancipated through the 13th Amendment that abolished slavery. In the south, Subjugated Moors, called slaves, were used to produce food and supplies that sustained the Confederate Army, while at the same time in the North, freed subjugated Moors served in the Union Army. About 20 out of 185,000 "subjugated Moor soldiers" were awarded the Medal of Honour for bravery.

IV. Dred Scott Decision

US Supreme Court 1856

DRED SCOTT v. SANFORD, 60 U.S. 393

MR. JUSTICE ROGER B. TANEY PRESIDING DECLARED THE PLAINTIFF, DRED SCOTT, IN ERROR.

"In the establishment of the several communities now the States of this Union, and in the formation of the Federal Government, the African WAS NOT DEEMED politically a PERSON. He was regarded as OWNED in every State in the Union as property merely, and as such was not and could not be a party or an actor, much less a peer in any compact or form of government established by the United States"

The Dred Scott case is the most fact proving case in US Court History regarding the true identity of the nappy headed, burnt skin people called "Slaves" in the Americas.

I. A free NEGRO of the African race, whose ancestors were brought to this country and sold as slaves, IS NOT A CITIZEN WITHIN the meaning of the Constitution of the United States. When the constitution was adopted, they WERE NOT regarded in ANY of the States as members of the community, which constituted the State, and were not numbered among its people.

A US citizen and an American Citizen are 2 different statuses. Free slaves, Free Negroes, Free Blacks all fall under US Corporate jurisdiction as these are misnomers. The concept of a "Free Black" or "Free Slaves" comes from their initial status as Moorish American. Lincoln called this land EGYPT OF THE WEST. In March 1865, Abraham Lincoln delivered his last address before his assassination. In his address he compared the Children of Israel under the evil Pharaoh enslaved in Egypt to the "so called" slaves under bondage by the European in the Americas. The Emancipation Proclamation was a transfer of ownership from the hands of chattel slave owners to the hands of the corporate state, as corporate property with granted privileges and NO rights. As a corporate citizen you are owned by the government whereas under

American Citizen status, YOU own the government and are the Master. This is also the difference between a DEMOCRACY and a REPUBLIC.

Slavery was instituted to fraudulently claim the Land and Birthright of Indigenous People. The fiction of race was created to as part of the Birthright theft to DIVIDE the people in order to separate their COMMON UNITY. As in the Dred Scott case, a freed negro slave cannot be a citizen because a Citizen is a different status than citizen. Just as Moor is a different status than N (n) egro, B (b) lack Person, C (c)oloured, African American or otherwise.

During the time of the Dred Scott case there were free Citizens called Moorish Americans of New Hampshire, New York, New Jersey and North Carolina. The Eagle seal represents the Caucasian European Order that was given permission by the Moorish Federal government already established to create a separate provisional government. The political government pushing a Democracy were the Europeans that infiltrated the US Republic, recognized by the Moorish government and secretly spread false History to institute and maintain slavery from a bureaucratic level. Politicians that owned slaves dumbed the people down to believing in the Democracy, not the Republic, and giving up their rights unknowingly. Governments are using Supreme Law to legally, not lawfully, take advantage of the people and give privileges disguised as rights.

"Not a single European nation, tribe or kingdom is responsible for the presence of "Blacks" in the Americas" (Barton 2001)

V. Too Cold For Blacks

The Treaty of Paris introduced English criminal and civil law. The transfer of power from the French to the British was the legal strengthening of slavery in Canada. **The Imperial Act encouraged immigration to British North America**. All European settlers took an oath of allegiance but Negro slaves weren't encouraged to go to BNA.

"It is known from experience that these persons brought up in servitude and slavery, want the assistance and protection of a master to make them happy; indeed to preserve them from penury and distress"- Colonel Morse

Black Sambo by Helen Campbell Bannerman was a Canadian classic and Canadians accepted the racial truths and historic half-truths without having daily contact with Melanin beings. The science of racial theorizing allowed Canada to bar "blacks" from Canada due to cold climate. We can see the extent of no rights for slaves since a "black" man Mathew A Henson survived the Arctic and co-discovered the North Pole with Admiral Robert Perry. Henson's triumph should have silenced contentions that "blacks" couldn't live in the cold but was ignored like the fact "blacks' had lived in Canada since the Adena people in 500 B.C. A Toronto attorney wrote an article about Africans in Canada did not hide his conviction that "blacks" didn't belong in Canadian society.

YOU BEEN HAD, TOOK AND BAMBOOZLED *OUT OF* YOUR BIRTHRIGHTS!

*"The Office of the Governor General, Canada's oldest continuing institution, is a thread that ties Canadians together. From Samuel de Champlain in 1608 to Viscount Monck in 1867 to Vincent Massey in 1952 to today's Governor General, the institution of Governor General dates back nearly 400 years. Canada is a parliamentary democracy and a constitutional monarchy. This means Canadians recognize The Queen as our

Head of State. Canada's Governor General carries out Her Majesty's duties in Canada on a daily basis and is Canada's de facto Head of State."- www.gg.ca

It is 2014 and we have become captives through USURPATION and trusting in a **de facto** Government using usury. We mentally invent a way to identify with our oppressors and this causes the demise we face as Melanin people and the hardships that are in and experience in the society we live. We live based on a conditioning of servitude to British Royalty and Melanin beings have been rationalizing their conditioning since coming out of physical chattel slavery. The conditioning has become accepted as a way of life without consideration of the result for our lack of thinking for ourselves. Slavery is alive and well through Spiriual Enslavement, which is scientific.

We were taught by our Master Ta'maure Teacher, Kaba Hiawatha Kamene, that SCIENCE is SEEN SPIRITUALITY and SPIRITUALITY IS UNSEEN SCIENCE. A slave owns nothing, even what's in his/her possession, belongs to the master. We have been duped into accepting the title of PERSON/citizen, and thinking that Corporate ENTITY called a PERSON is you, the Sovereign, since your picture and signature is identified with that ALL CAPS NAME on all your identification and statements of accounts. The Government is practicing fraud as it knows it is a corporation and can only deal with CORPORATE ENTITIES, but due to our ignorance and misinterpretation, Moors are labeled and have accepted titles that delude to slavery, and Moors claim to be those misnomers that delude to slavery, when they are **NOT** those misnomers, which is fraud. So instead of charging you with fraud for impersonating a company, the Canadian Government decides to tax the corporation, through another CORPORATION called REVENUE CANADA, when in actuality the corporation gets taxed through your sovereign being, not the ALL CAPS CORPORATION. The controllers of the system have set it up so that the only way for the sovereign to access the industrial goods and services of the nation is through a nominal third party, a stunt double, a dummy, a public corporation of one, a coloured juristic person, the straw man - a avenue through which said goods and services may be relayed. YOU MUST REMEMBER, **YOU**, the Sovereign, are not beholden to the straw man, since you didn't create it, but, the sovereign is the one responsible for discharging the liability associated with the "benefits" that come to you, the sovereign, in the name of the straw man.   All "income" is "corporate income," and the straw man is a created public corporation. Failing to establish sovereignty in law allows you NOT to hold title to anything, to NO legal capacity and become and remain a permanent debtor and will lose in any dispute with the system. Before any session goes forward in a court of law, jurisprudence says the courts must identify Status, Jurisdiction/Venue then Adjudication. Those who are Wards of the state, persons, citizens, negro, coloured, black, African, Ethiopian, Trinidadian, Jamaican and other misnomers give up their status and jurisdiction rights and are usually adjudicated, which is law practiced fraudulently. Nationality is a right, not a privilege, which is upheld by the Constitution of Canada, which is a fraud since the Constitution of Canada is an ACT. The Canadian Bill of Rights recognizes that human rights and fundamental freedoms is not a privilege.

"The Parliament of Canada, affirming that the Canadian Nation is founded upon principles that acknowledge the supremacy of God, the dignity and worth of the human person and the position of the family in a society of free men and free institutions"- Preamble, Canadian Bill of Rights

VI. Our Authority

We have a right, as Moorish Americans living on our land commonly called North America—not the Corporate banner of Canada—to life, liberty and the RIGHT not to be deprived thereof except by due process of law. We have the right to freedom of conscience and religion, speech, equality before the law and protection of the law. The wordplay game is the important implicating factor in Melanin beings not getting the rights they deserve as free will sovereign and getting the freedom they have been fighting for so long. This is the same word play game the heads of churches play in Religion, by getting Melanin beings to ignorantly accepting lies as truth to come to a false understanding. Melanin beings, through this misunderstanding, miss the point all together, or intentionally ignore the facts. The person/citizen is **not** a free-will sovereign, that person/citizen is a corporation or a fictitious entity also called the straw man (refer to wizard of Oz movie). This corporation was created by the Crown of a Province through your birth certificate, with your family name on it, spelt grammatically incorrect as a false birth cert. name. The Crown of Canada uses that False BIRTH CERT. NAME and attaches a S.I.N # to IT, which allows the Crown to claim part ownership of the PERSON, that is actually a corporation. The Province also uses and attaches the drivers licence as I.D for the false birth cert. name person.

All card-like documents given to you by the Government are contracts. The driver's license is for corporate commerce activity, and transfer and travel of commercial goods on highways. The drivers' license is being instituted and used as I.D when it is not an I.D card! It is a card for corporations, doing business in a corporation on paper, and being that you are not a corporation, and not doing business, you should not need a driver's license. Another point that must be made clear is that if you are a Moor that lives until death, and they want to use the license as I.D, it CAN'T have an expiry date, if our identification doesn't expire. If the drivers' license is used as I.D, that instrument will take away and/or supremely violate your nationality and birth rights. Most politicians and court officers are masons in lodges and know this Truth about Law and Government and its workings. They wear a fez with a tacked tassel, while ours is not tacked. The fact they got the fez from us is the secret they can't reveal.

Figure 2: The Triple Crown is also a fez!!!!

VII. The Power of Persuasion

We are under the impression that THEY are doing something to us when it is us, in not being knowledgeable, allowing ourselves to be taken advantage of. A Moorish American is a free-standing, independent sovereign who's right to exist and act is inherent by nature. A free will being is created with Inherent, Inborn, Ingrained, Innate, Instinctive, Intuitive, and Inalienable Natural Rights of freewill, and until they are balanced among all members of the one Human Family, there is no true Love, Truth, Peace, Freedom and Justice! Inalienable Natural Rights include to Protect against Initiatory Physical Force, Coercion and Fraud, to Protect Self-governance, to Protect against Environmental and Physical Harm, to Protect Justly-acquired Personal Property, to Protect one's Freewill to Travel, Trade and Associate with others, to Protect one's Expression on Public Issues, to protect one's Right to Participate Equally and Vote Directly on Public Issues, to Protect one's Right to dissociate from any Principle, Policy, Program, Practice or Person, to Protect against any human-contaminated Air, Water, Soil and Food, to Protect Equal Access to Public Places and Public Information, and to Protect Open, Transparent settlement of Differences with others. Our acting power is not based upon or answerable to any other person or any other person's creation. The neglect of a sovereign's Nationality and Birth rights by governmental ordinances is carelessness and ignorance on behalf of the SOVEREIGN. As an individual with natural rights are protected, so is all life and the earth protected for the highest good of all.

"One of the qualifications for one to be a Mason is to be a FREE BORN, meaning no slave ancestry. BLACKMEN proclaim they are descendants of slaves. Moors proclaim their Ancestors as being prisoners of war, kidnapped and victims of genocide. Moors also proclaim their forefathers and foremothers as being the original torchbearers of civilization, thus , there is nothing a MASON with a BOUND tassel on a fez, who is bound to 32 and in some cases 33 degrees can tell a Moor who is inherently 360 and in select cases 720 degrees"- Amir: Heru Ranesi El

VIII. Canadian Common Wealth

Canada is one of sixteen Commonwealth realms, all of which share the same person as their respective sovereign. **Commonwealth realm** is any one of 16 sovereign states within the Commonwealth of Nations with Elizabeth II as their respective monarch. The **Commonwealth of Nations**, usually known as **the Commonwealth** and sometimes as the **British Commonwealth**, is currently a voluntary association of 53 independent sovereign states, most of which are former British colonies.

THE COMMONWEALTH is an international organization through which countries with diverse social, political, and economic backgrounds co-operate within a framework of common values and goals, outlined in the Singapore Declaration. The **Singapore Declaration of Commonwealth Principles** was a declaration issued by the assembled Heads of Government of the Commonwealth of Nations, setting out the core political values that would form the main part of the Commonwealth's membership criteria. The **Harare Commonwealth Declaration** was a declaration of the Commonwealth of Nations, setting out the Commonwealth's core principles and values, detailing the Commonwealth's membership criteria, and redefining and reinforcing its purpose. The Declaration reaffirms those principles to which it was committed in 1971: world peace and support for the United Nations; individual liberty and egalitarianism; opposition to racism; opposition to colonialism; the eradication of poverty, ignorance, disease, and economic inequality; free trade; institutional cooperation; multilateralism; and the rejection of international coercion.

THE QUEEN, because of Canada's federal system, is represented at both levels of GOVERNMENT, federally by the GOVERNOR GENERAL and in each province by a federally appointed LIEUTENANT-GOVERNOR. The monarch appoints the Governor General on the advice of the Canadian Prime Minister. All officials, from the prime minister to a collector of taxes, are under the same responsibility for any act done without legal justification as every other citizen is, reflecting the principle of the Rule Of Law, which is also part of Canadian constitutional law. The rule of law is an underlying constitutional principle requiring government to be conducted according to law and making all public officers answerable for their acts in the ordinary courts.

ADMINISTRATIVE LAW is one of the 3 basic areas of public law dealing with the relationship between government and its citizens, the other 2 being CONSTITUTIONAL LAW and CRIMINAL LAW. We can also add MARITIME Law and ADMIRALTY Law, as these spheres of law deal with contracts, vessels, sea space, land space etc. Administrative law is based on the principle that government action, whatever form it takes, must be legal and lawful, and that citizens who are affected by unlawful acts of government officials must have effective remedies. Criminal law is a body of law that prohibits certain kinds of conduct and imposes sanctions for unlawful behavior. A number of federal offences and offences under provincial statutes (liquor and highway control offences) and municipal bylaws (parking tickets, pet control) are not criminal offences in the true sense, but are generally processed through the courts in the same general manner as criminal offences. A very important development in Canadian criminal procedure is the inclusion of the Canadian Charter of Rights and Freedoms into the Constitution Act of 1982. Although the Charter does not set out any procedural rules, it does provide many of the principles that procedural rules must follow.

These principles include the Constitution Acts of 1867 and 1982 and other documents that make up the Constitution of Canada, federal and provincial statutes related to constitutional matters, orders-in-council, letters patent and proclamations. The Constitution Act, 1982 provides for the Constitution of Canada to include the Canada Act of 1982 and the Constitution Act of 1982, legislative texts and decrees included in Appendix I of the latter Act, and the modifications to these legislative texts and decrees. Canada has inherited the Bill of Rights of 1689, the Act of Settlement of 1701 and various other British statutes and charters.

Other sources of constitutional law include case law which is the interpretation of the Constitution by the courts, which is just as important as the Constitution itself, especially in Canada, where statutes are subject to judicial review for their constitutionality. The Constitution overrides any incompatible provision of any piece of legislation. Judiciaries are judges of the courts, collectively and also the branch of government in which judicial power is vested. Judges are public officers of the court appointed to preside and administer the law in a court of justice. The Constitution Act of 1867 provides for the establishment and operation of Canada's professional judiciary.

It gave the federal government exclusive lawmaking power over Criminal Law and Criminal Procedure but not over the establishment of criminal courts while it gives the provinces lawmaking power over the administration of justice in each province.

CHARTER OF RIGHTS AND FREEDOMS

Prior to the Proclamation of the Canadian Charter of Rights and Freedoms, the law of civil liberties in Canada was not disciplined by a constitutionally entrenched Charter of Rights and Freedoms. The Charter was affected by this history, as rights were designed not only in contemplation of an intelligent civil liberties system, but also bargained off against various demands by provincial premiers. The Charter is meant to decrease powers of both levels of government by ensuring both federal and provincial laws respect Charter rights, under Section 32:

"32. (1) This Charter applies

a) to the Parliament and government of Canada in respect of all matters within the authority of Parliament including all matters relating to the Yukon Territory and Northwest Territories; and

b) to the legislature and government of each province in respect of all matters within the authority of the legislature of each province.

(2) Notwithstanding subsection (1), section 15 shall not have effect until three years after this section comes into force."

The relationship between federalism and the Charter is directly dealt with in Section 31:

31. Nothing in this Charter extends the legislative powers of any body or authority. In which it is made clear neither the federal nor provincial governments gain powers under the Charter.

GOVERNMENT "AUTHORITY"

The Courts found that the "authority" of government consisted of all laws created by the three branches of government (executive, legislative, and administrative), as well as any rules, or regulations created by "government actors". A government actor consists of institutions for which the government has statutory authority to exercise substantial control over the day-to-day operations, policy-making, and as well provides substantial funding for the institution. The Supreme Court held that the Charter equally applies to courts as well. In Canada, the head of state can, in exceptional circumstances, protect Parliament and the people against a Prime Minister and Ministers who may forget that "minister" means "servant," to the Queen but may try to make themselves masters. Although not "laws" enforceable in the courts, such principles are of importance to effective constitutional government. The Supreme Court stated in 1981 during the patriation (Patriation refers to making the constitution amendable by Canada only, with no role for the Parliament of the United Kingdom to play in the amending process) of the Constitution that "constitutional conventions plus constitutional law equal the total constitution of the country. The people, the free will men and women living within the national boundaries, are sovereign and are subservient only to Creator God. The people are not to be considered as a 'crew', as indicated by the term 'People'. The People choose representatives to form a government (not a corporation) to do only that which they can't do individually or collectively. 'Bodies politic', political organizations, must remain unincorporated. The Law of the Land is the negative Golden Rule. Social justice arises from the Positive to Golden Rule. The 'enforcement' of law only applies the negative Law. The positive Law must remain a totally moral responsibility and accountability to where you domicile and travel. Law enforcement remains in the hands of the People through the jury system (jury of my own peers) Judges must only be 'referees' and helpful advisors to the jury in matters of procedure, conduct and protocol. The Law of the Sea and international relations derives from Maritime Law, also known as Admiralty Law when applied to military matters. This is why we will see the Canada flag with the gold fringe in the courts. This proves the FRAUD as Flag law says anything added to a National flag defaces it. Such a system of individual freedom threatening laws must remain outside the nation's boundaries, or be very specific and with full revelation when affecting people through terms of an international contract.

  The constitution is a contract between the People and their Government. It is the job description and the limitations of policing power of the government. Indigenous rights and freedoms must take precedent over their community, with de-jure due process of law. It is this which prohibits government from confiscating the primary right of 'life', and the supportive rights of 'liberty', property, and property, not the pursuit of happiness.

IX. Moor's Head

The Moor's head is not rare in European heraldry. It still appears today in the arms of Sardinia and Corsica, as well as in the blazons of various noble families. Italian heraldry, however, usually depicts the Moor wearing a white band, or diadem, around his head instead of a crown, indicating a slave who has been freed; whereas in German heraldry the Moor is shown wearing a crown. The Moor's head is common in the Bavarian tradition and is known as the *caput Ethiopicum* or *the Moor of Freising*. In Christian tradition the Magi, also known as the Three Wise Men, The Three Kings, or Kings from the east. The Magi depicted as the Moor was Zenone da Verona (about 300 - 371 or 300 - 380) and was either an early Christian Bishop or martyr. On June 2, 2007, for the first time, a "black" Canadian played the role of OTHELLO at the Stratford Festival. Philip Akin was the Melanin being that played this historic role. "Interpretations of Othello's origins as "Black" were current as of the 1930s, when a performance of the play was banned in a southern U.S. state due to the prejudices against representing an idealized, inter-racial love. So the Moors are identified even in Shakespeare!!!!

Love, Truth, Peace, Freedom and Justice are meshed in every fiber of the Moorish American from our Constitution and By-Laws, to our Circle 7 Holy Koran to the Moorish Flag, from the Moorish American Prayer to the Proclamations and Moorish Seal. It is expected that the Five Highest Principles ever known to Man to be personified in the hearts and minds of every Moorish American and in turn manifest in the hearts and minds of humanity as a whole.

"The Spaniards did not understand that they had put out the brightest light Spain would ever see. For centuries Spain had been the center of civilization, the seat of the arts and sciences of learning and every form of refined enlightenment. No country had ever come close to the cultivated dominion of the Moors. Until this day the handworks of the Moors still stand strong, leaving Spain and the West indebted forever to the once colorful, dashing, intelligent Conquering Moors"- (Gorham Bey and Rosser El 2000).

Biblio-/Discography

Sovereignty. Performed by Amir Ali El. n.d.

American Heritage Dictionary. Boston: Houghton Mifflin, 1969.

Amir: Heru Ranesi El, G.S. *What Shall We Call Him?* Atlanta, GA: Moorish Science Temple of America, 2010.

Ancient American Magazine. "Issue 17." n.d.

Barton, Paul Alfred. *A History of the African-Olmecs: Black Civilizations of America from Prehistoric Times to the Present Era.* Bloomington, IN: 1st Book Library, 2001.

Warnings from the Prophet Noble Drew Ali. Performed by Hakim Bey. n.d.

British Parliament. "Act of Union." British Parliament, 1840.

Moorish Science 101. Performed by C. Freeman El. n.d.

Gorham Bey, E, and D. Rosser El. *Who Were The Negroes Before Slaves.* Hyattsville, MD: Moorish Pub, 2000.

Holy Day Service. Performed by Grand Body of the Prophet's Temple in Chicago. n.d.

Moors Conquest of Spain. Performed by Kaba Hiawatha Kamene. n.d.

Science is Seen, Spirituality is Unseen. Performed by Kaba Hiawatha Kamene. n.d.

Kaplan, Sydney. *The Black Presence in the Era of the American Revolution 1770-1800.* New York: New York Graphic Society, 1973.

Noble Drew Ali, T. *The Holy Koran of the Moorish Science Temple of America Circle 7.* Chicago: Moorish Guide Publishing, 1928.

Robertson, John Ross. *Robertson's landmarks of Toronto; a collection of historical sketches of the old town of York from 1792 until 1833, and of Toronto from 1834 to 1893 .* Toronto: Toronto Evening Telegram, 1894.

Services, Ontario Ministry of Government & Consumer. *The Black Canadian Experience in Ontario 1834-1914; Flight Freedom Foundation.* December 28, 2011. http://www.archives.gov.on.ca/en/explore/online/black_history/index.aspx (accessed August 8, 2014).

Shabazz Bey, Umar. *We Are the Washitaw*. Indigenous Concepts, 1996.

Smith, T. Wilson. *The Slave in Canda: A Collection of the Nova Scotia Historical Society for the Years 1896-1898, Vol. X*. Halifax, N.S.: Nova Scotia Printing Company, 1899.

"Statutes Revision Act." n.d.

Constitutional Fold of Government. Directed by Taj Tarik Bey. Performed by Taj Tarik Bey. n.d.

—. *Moors of the Roundtable Civic Lessons*. New York: R.V. Bey Publications, 1996.

—. *Nigger Industries, I & II*. New York: R.V. Bey Publications, n.d.

The Wizard of Oz. Directed by Norman Taurog. 1939.

"The British North America Act." 1867.

The Holy Bible. n.d.

Walker, James W. St. G. *The Black Loyalists: The Search for a Promised Land in Nova Scotia and Sierra Leone 1783-1870* . Toronto: University of Toronto Press, Scholarly Publishing Division, 1993.

Winks, Robin W. *The Blacks in Canada: A History*. Montreal: Mcgill Queens Univ Pr; 2, 1997.

Index

A

Act of Settlement, 1701 · 28
Act of Union · 5
Adena · 3, 21
Admiralty Law · 30
Akin, Philip · 31
Albany · *See* Underground Railroad
apprenticeships · 12
Asia Soor · 4

B

Bay of Fundy · 5
Beringia · 2
Bill of Rights, 1689 · 28
birthright theft · 20
Black Codes, 1865 · 14
Black loyalist · 14
Black Loyalists · 14
branding · 16
British North America Act · 5, 7
British North America Act, 1867 · 5
Buffalo · *See* Undergound Railroad

C

Canada Act, 1982 · 28
Canadian Bill of Rights · 23
Canadian Charter of Rights and Freedoms · 28

Charter of Rights and Freedoms · 29
Civil War · 14
code noir, 1685 · 14
Code Noir, 1685 · 16
confederation · 7
Constitution Act, 1982 · 28
Constitution Acts, 1867 · 28
Constitutional Act · 5
corporate citizen · 19
Corsica · 31

D

da Verona, Zenone · 31
Danes · 3
Douglass, Frederick · 11
driver's license · 24

E

Egypt of the West\ · 19
Elizabeth II · 5
Empire Washitaw de Dugdamoundya · 2, *See* Washitaw
estate · 7

F

Free blacks · 14
Free White · 18
Freedman's Relief Association · 17
Freedman's Bureau · 18

freewill · 26
fur trade · 3

G

Governor General · 6
Great Lakes · 2
    Atomic Lakes · 2
    Erie · 2
    Huron · 2
    Michigan · 2
    Ontario · 2
    Superior · 2
Guadeloupe · 4

H

Harare Commonwealth Declaration · 27
Henson, Mathew A · 21
heraldry · 31
Hudson's Bay Company · 3

I

Imperial Act · 21
Inalienable Natural Rights · 26
indentured · 14
Indentured servants · *See* Indentured

J

Jarvis Collegiate · 11
Jay, John · 13

K

Klondike Gold Rush · 5
Knights Templars · 13
Ku Klux Klan · 18

L

Lacus Atomus · *See* Atomic Lakes

M

Maritime Law · 30
Martinique · 4
Metis Provisional Government · 13
minister · 30
Moorish Empire · *See* Moors
Moors · 12, 16
Moroccan Empire · *See* Moors
mounds · 2, 3

N

Naturalization Act, 1870 · 18
new france · 14
New France · 4
Northwest Amexem · 2
Nova Scotia · 5

O

Ohio River · 3

P

Parliament · 6
patriation · 30
People, The · 30
Prophet Noble Drew Ali · 2
pyramids · 2

Q

Quebec resolutions · 7
Queen Anne's War · 3

R

Residuary Powers · 9
Rochester · *See* Undergound Railroad
Rule Of Law · 27

S

Sardinia · 31
Scandinavian · 3
Scott, Dred · 19, 20
Seven Years' War · 4
Singapore Declaration · 27
Slave Trade Act, 1807 · 12
Slavery Abolition Act · 12
Slavery Abolition Act, 1833 · 12
sovereign · 22, 26
spiritual enslavement · 22
St. Lawrence · 5
States Rights · 9
Statutes Law (Repeals) Act, 1998 · 12
Statutes Revision Act · 6
Subjugated Moors · 18
Swedes · 3
Syracuse · *See* Undergound Railroad

T

Treaty of London, 1794 · 12
Treaty of Paris, 1783 · 3, 12, 21
Treaty of Peace and Friendship, 1787 · 12
trick contracts · 14

U

Underground Railroad · 11, 12
US Securities and Exchange Commission · 9

V

Victoria · 6

W

wards · 23
Washitaw · 2
Wisconsin · 3

Y

Yukon · 3
Yukon Territory · 5

Other Titles Available from Califa Media Publishing ™

Moorish Children's Guide to History and Culture

Moorish Jewels: Emerald Ed

Moors in America

Moslem Girls' Training Guide a.k.a. The Sisters' Auxiliary Handbook

Nationality, the Order of the Day

Noble Drew Ali Plenipotentiaries

Official Proclamation of Real Moorish American Nationality

Who Stole the Fez, Moors or Shriners?

Califa Uhuru Series

Vol. 1:   Holy Koran of the Moorish Holy Temple of Science, Circle 7

Vol. 2: "I'm Going to Repeat Myself.":   A Collection of Artifacts Authored by Noble Prophet Drew Ali and the M.S.T. of A.

Vol. 3:   Mysteries of the Silent Brotherhood of the East a.ka. The Red Book, a.k.a. Sincerity

Vol. 4:   Califa Uhuru; A Collection of Literature from the Moorish Science Temple of America

www.ingramcontent.com/pod-product-compliance
Lightning Source LLC
Chambersburg PA
CBHW030202100526

44592CB00009B/413